Television Production Today!

Teacher's Resource Book

With Sample Forms

James D. Kirkham

 NATIONAL TEXTBOOK COMPANY • Lincolnwood, Illinois U.S.A.

Contents

PART 1

Introduction

The Text

Television Production Today! is designed to support students in the preparation and presentation of television programming. Its aim is to show students how to use television effectively to send messages. The text provides guided, simplified experiences for those who want to learn what is involved in producing programs in the classroom, on closed circuit cable, or on public or commercial station. All of the activities can be accomplished in a small, modestly equipped studio.

Television Production Today! is based on the philosophy that students learn by doing. They learn the tools, techniques, and terminology of television production by producing programs. It is only after actual hands-on experience that students understand and appreciate the process of television production. *Television Production Today!* was formerly *Televising Your Message.* The new edition uses the same teaching philosophy as did the previous edition.

Television Production Today! is carefully planned to support both conceptual learning and skill development. Concepts are reinforced by both individual and group activities in sections that follow each chapter. *Videolabs* are creative laboratory activities that provide actual experience in production techniques. The activities are designed to involve the entire class. *Take Two* sections are opportunities to evaluate, discuss, and extend chapter content. Additional text features include unique and inexpensive production ideas called *Economy Notes,* suggested additional reading lists, a useful *Glossary* and a detailed *Index.* Sample scripts, storyboards, and floor plans are also provided to help guide students through the learning process.

Television Production Today! is organized into eight chapters.

Chapter One, Viewing the Message, examines how the growth in technology affects TV viewing and reports on the factors that determine viewing habits.

Chapter Two, Assessing the Medium, discusses the types of media that students can use to transmit messages and the importance of audience analysis.

Chapter Three, Visualizing the Message, is a heavily illustrated section that focuses on the variety of cameras available and the types of lighting used.

Chapter Four, Sounding the Message, discusses various types of sound equipment, performers' use of microphones, and principles of radio broadcasting.

Chapter Five, Verbalizing the Message, examines the importance of scripts and discusses the importance of obtaining permission to use copyrighted materials.

Chapter Six, Producing the Message, discusses the importance of the production team and explains the role of each team member.

Chapter Seven, Taping the Message, reports on the variety of available taping equipment and explains the process of assemble and insert edits.

Chapter Eight, Considering Careers in Television, discusses the range of career opportunities in the television industry and related jobs that utilize television production skills.

This Resource Book

This *Teacher's Resource Book With Sample Forms* is designed to help the instructor use *Television Produc-*

1

tion Today! to its fullest. The *Book* supplements the text and supports the development of the course. Together, the *Book* and text offer the instructor a complete teaching package.

Like the text, the *Teacher's Resource Book With Sample Forms* provides simplified activities that can be accomplished in a small studio. The activities are designed for a class size of about twenty students. This allows students to take turns participating as crew members. The actual hands-on experience students gain will help them to better understand the process of television production. If the class size is larger, it may be more convenient to break the class in smaller groups.

Many of the simplified experiences included in this *Book* have been gained through twelve years of experience in teaching television production. The activities have been constantly modified to fit the changing needs of students and to incorporate new ideas and modern technology.

Additional features include crossword puzzles, chapter-by-chapter tests, script forms, and complete instructions on how the forms and handouts can be used in a variety of ways.

The *Teacher's Resource Book With Sample Forms* is divided into eight parts.

Part One, the Introduction, gives an overview of *Television Production Today!* and this *Book*.

Part Two provides formative guidelines for evaluating student achievement and identifying student progress for each text chapter.

Part Three includes a variety of approaches to instruction and offers ideas for use of television production in various academic areas.

Part Four offers help in course planning. A list of organizations, publications, and companies is provided to help the instructor gather additional materials for the course.

Part Five offers a variety of assignments and activities for each text chapter. The activities can be used either as additional laboratory experiences to supplement the Videolab sections of the text, or as substitute exercises.

Part Six includes a crossword puzzle for each text chapter. The puzzles offer students an interesting way to learn key terms. This section also features sample forms: a floor plan, storyboard outline, audio/video storyboard script, and a video script. Activity materials for assignments are also provided. The forms and handouts have been formatted for convenient photocopying and distribution.

Part Seven includes a Performance Evaluation form that the instructor can use to encourage the development of critical evaluation skills. The form can be utilized in a variety of ways, for a variety of performances—both professional and in the classroom. In addition, a written test and an essay question for each chapter is provided in this section to help measure student progress. The materials in this part are formatted for easy photocopying and distribution.

Part Eight includes answer keys to all crossword puzzles and chapter tests. Because answers on essay questions will vary, points and comments are provided on what students should be expected to cover.

PART 2

Behavioral Objectives

Your use of *Television Production Today!* will depend on your expectations of the class. Is it to be a performance-oriented course geared to the needs of actors, public speakers, guitar players, and folk singers? Is it to be a technical course designed to train beginning engineers, graphic artists, and television production people? Is it to be a programming unit intended to bring about social change? Is it designed to change the viewing habits and criteria of students? The variety of activities in *Television Production Today!* and in this *Book* allow considerable flexibility in course planning.

Which chapters you choose to assign to students will be determined by your selection of behavioral objectives for your particular course. If a teacher is to be held accountable for learning achieved by students, he or she must have 1) knowledge of the objectives, both cognitive and affective, and 2) evidence of student awareness and achievement. This section contains both behavioral objectives and guidelines to assist you in assessing student progress in achieving learning goals. They are presented chapter by chapter.

You may find it helpful to consult Bloom's *Taxonomy of Educational Objectives* and Magner's *Preparing Behavioral Objectives* when you plan your instructional goals.

Chapter 1   Viewing the Message

Behavioral Objectives

1. The student will calculate and evaluate his or her TV viewing habits.

2. The student will be able to recognize the newer tools for measuring television viewing and the importance of ratings.

3. The student will be able to identify differences in advertising rates for television and radio based upon the size of the market.

4. The student will be able to evaluate the newer technology and its effect on broadcasting.

5. The student will be able to identify the difference between local origination and public access channels of local cable TV systems.

6. The student will be able to identify the major milestones in broadcasting history.

Evidence of Student Achievement and Response

1. The student will produce a one-minute radio "spot" highlighting a significant person or event in broadcast history.

2. The student will be able to explain the difference between public access and LO programming and should take the access course and use this channel.

3. The student will be able to explain how modern video has influenced network television programming.

Chapter 2   Assessing the Medium

Behavioral Objectives

1. The student should be able to evaluate the process and the product of television.

2. The student should learn to recognize effective patterns of communication appropriate to the medium.

3. The student should exhibit critical listening behavior as a viewer and as a listener.

4. The student should become aware of the factors affecting his or her choice of television programs.

5. The student should become aware of the effects of television viewing.

6. The student should be able to recognize propaganda techniques used in mass communication.

7. The student will be able to identify new technology including cable TV, video discs, and recorders.

Evidence of Student Achievement and Response

1. The student will be familiar with specialized television terminology and will use it when appropriate in oral and written assignments.

2. The student will comment on current happenings in the field of broadcasting such as political campaigns, new techniques for commercials, and renewal or cancellation of program contracts.

3. The student will comment on rating services and their polls.

4. The student will evaluate and discuss programs he or she has seen.

5. The student will write to networks and sponsors expressing opinions and concerns.

6. The student will suggest program ideas and class activities appropriate to the classroom or studio.

7. The student will comment on the importance of television news to a station.

8. The student will be able to identify techniques used in a TV newscast to attract viewers.

9. The student will be able to identify all the visual elements used in a television newscast.

Chapter 3 Visualizing the Message

Behavioral Objectives

1. The student should be able to use cameras and related television equipment with some proficiency.

2. The student should be able to identify and prepare graphics for use on camera.

3. The student should know the most appropriate means of displaying graphics and properties.

4. The student should be able to convey ideas through the effective use of graphics.

5. The student should be able to identify the basic lighting instruments and their purposes.

6. The student should be able to select two-dimensional graphics having the correct aspect ratio.

7. The student should be able to operate switching equipment when two or more cameras are being used.

8. The student should be able to prepare floor plans for efficient and effective camera movement.

9. The student should be able to translate ideas into a visual package.

10. The student, using 3 point lighting, should be able to prepare suitable lighting plots with available equipment.

11. The student should be able to utilize audio equipment used in a TV production.

12. The student will be able to work with others as he or she is a member of a team that is needed to create a TV production.

13. The student will be able to operate portable TV videotape recording equipment so that field recordings can be made.

Evidence of Student Achievement and Response

1. The student will use appropriate terminology in referring to studio equipment and activities.

2. The student will arrange objects and people for the best possible picture composition.

3. The student will select camera shots that require little correction.

4. The student will prepare shot lists for his or her own use.

5. The student will discuss the visual images and shots of a television program.

6. The student will comment on the differences between classroom and studio productions.

7. The student will prepare his or her own gray scale for more effective shading and lighting.

8. The student will select the appropriate lighting equipment for each function.

9. The student will use a light meter to ascertain lighting conditions.

10. The student will request opportunities to practice with cameras to determine capabilities and limitations.

11. The student will prepare lighting plots for classroom and studio productions.

12. The student will discuss special lighting effects he or she has observed on commercial television.

13. The student will respond with speed and accuracy to commands to dolly, truck, or pan the camera; to rack lenses; to focus; to frame effective picture composition.

14. The student will be able to create simple storyboards showing that he or she can think in pictures rather than verbiage.

15. The student will be able to create radio and TV scripts used for productions.

Chapter 4   Sounding the Message
Behavioral Objectives

1. The student should become aware of musical moods and the aesthetic and psychological role they play in radio and television programs.

2. The student should be able to ride gain on volume controls for clarity and aesthetic effect.

3. The student should be able to select microphones suitable to acoustical conditions.

4. The student should be able to make simple acoustical adjustments to create live and dead pickup conditions.

5. The student should know the characteristics of the most common types of microphones.

6. The student should be able to use a microphone effectively when performing.

7. The student should be able to communicate a message by sound alone.

8. The student should be able to respond to the nonverbal signals and cues used in a radio program.

9. The student should be able to select and improvise simple sound effects.

10. The student should be able to compare tapes, cassettes, and cartridges and select the one most appropriate for his or her purpose.

11. The student will create radio commercials using voice, music, and sound effects.

Evidence of Student Achievement and Response

1. The student will use the appropriate specialized terminology referring to acoustical properties, microphones, and the broadcasting of sound.

2. The student will select the correct microphone for a broadcast.

3. The student will refer to the technical descriptive terms of the mikes he or she sees being used by performers on television, such as lapel, lavaliere, and boom.

4. The student will position and operate microphones correctly for recording and/or broadcasting.

5. The student will operate pot and key controls correctly.

Chapter 5   Verbalizing the Message
Behavioral Objectives

1. The student should be able to recognize and follow broadcast regulations.

2. The student should be able to prepare scripts according to the established format.

3. The student will understand the need for a script.

4. The student should be able to communicate to the performers and to the director the message that he or she wishes the script to convey.

5. The student should be able to follow a script prepared by someone else.

6. The student should be able to back time a script and mark it for the director.

7. The student should be able to identify the differences between a scripted show and a partially scripted show and should be able to select the one more appropriate for his or her purpose.

8. The student should be familiar with copyright regulations.

Evidence of Student Achievement and Response

1. The student will prepare satisfactory scripts.

2. The student will mark scripts with the appropriate symbols for the crew and director.

3. The student will interpret and follow script directions correctly when functioning as a member of the production crew.

4. The student will select subject matter that meets the standards set by broadcast regulations.

5. The student will assume responsibility for clearance of copyrighted material used in all scripts.

6. The student will give commands concisely, using the least amount of words.

7. The student will complete the floor plans for productions.

Chapter 6   Producing the Message

Behavioral Objectives

1. The student should be able to use and respond to the terminology used by television production crews.

2. The student should be able to plan and organize the elements of a television production.

3. The student should be able to work effectively as a member of a television crew.

4. The student should be able to operate the equipment in the television studio as part of a production team.

5. The student should be able to evaluate the performance of other members of the production team.

6. The student should demonstrate interpersonal skills that enable him or her to work efficiently with other members of the television production team.

7. The student will be able to react effectively and competently in a tension-filled production as a TV director.

8. The student will be able to think ahead, so that problems in TV productions will be anticipated.

Evidence of Student Achievement and Response

1. The student will refer to other members of the production crew by position rather than by name (e.g., *floor manager* rather than Carmen, *boom operator* rather than Chris, *camera 2* rather than Alvina).

2. The student will respond quickly and accurately to the instructions of the technical director.

3. The student will assume full responsibility for the duties of his or her crew position.

4. The student will see that equipment is protected through careful operation and preventive maintenance.

5. The student will assume responsibility for striking the set.

Chapter 7   Taping the Message

Behavioral Objectives

1. The student should be able to operate the available videotape recorders.

2. The student should be able to identify and correct simple errors in operation such as improper threading and reel in the wrong position.

3. The student should exhibit some proficiency in recording, playing back, and erasing taped material.

4. The student should be able to transport portable equipment without damage to the equipment.

5. The student should be able to keep the necessary written records and to maintain production logs.

6. The student should be able to "spot" a specific part of a script on the tape.

7. The student should be able to shoot a remote sequence on videotape, white balance the camera, shoot wild video necessary for inserts, and operate the video camera for a remote telecast.

8. If editing equipment is available, the student should be able to edit sequence shots in remote locations to create a story or a news interview. He or she will be able to use assemble and insert edits in the final production.

Evidence of Student Achievement and Response

1. The student will discuss with others the advantages and disadvantages of different kinds of recording equipment.

2. The student will protect tapes and equipment by placing them in suitable areas away from heat sources and dust.

3. During playback sessions the student will discuss with increasing awareness the flaws resulting from poor taping techniques or faulty equipment.

4. The student will discuss with others instant replay techniques they have observed on commercial telecasts.

Chapter 8   Considering Careers in Television

Behavioral Objectives

1. The student should become familiar with the many facets of television.

2. The student should become familiar with the many different careers in the television industry.

3. The student should be able to relate his or her personal qualifications to the requirements of the television industry.

4. The student should be able to locate sources of reliable information about employment in the television industry.

5. The student should be able to compare and contrast the activities of commercial and educational broadcasting facilities.

6. The student will have explored career opportunities in industrial and cable TV, as well as commercial broadcast positions.

Evidence of Student Achievement and Response

1. The student will talk with persons employed in the television industry.

2. The student will seek opportunities to observe on-the-job activities in the industry.

3. The student will discuss with his or her adviser personal qualifications for various careers in television and its related fields.

4. The student will discuss studio assignments as they compare with similar positions in the television industry.

5. The student will ask questions about college studio facilities and job opportunities for college students.

6. The student will investigate formal training opportunities in colleges and in vocational schools.

7. The student will have experienced each job in television production for commercial, industrial, and cable TV programs.

PART 3

Correlated Multidisciplinary Experiences

For every subject matter there is a message to be communicated. It is not the role of the television teacher to tamper with that message, but the television teacher can serve the entire school community. "Media services" is a term chosen by many who teach television production to affirm the principle that television equipment is a tool to serve the needs of all the instructional staff. Teachers of numerous academic areas will find that *Television Production Today!* includes activities and information useful in their courses.

Art

Teachers of art may offer Chapter 3, "Visualizing the Message," as a reference for general principles of visualization. Preparing the graphics suggested for television and checking them on camera for effectiveness can help prepare students for commercial art assignments.

Counseling

The techniques for television production discussed in *Television Production Today!* can assist in several of these counseling areas.

1. *College information:* A counselor could videotape information about available scholarships with charts, diagrams, graphs, and application forms. An instructor who has worked closely with administering entrance and placement examinations could discuss questions students are likely to have. The tapes could be played at the request of a student who might need the information when the counselor is committed to other assignments.

Interviews with college representatives, charts showing costs and entrance requirements, or slides of campus scenes might be videotaped and made available to students as they need them.

2. *Course election:* Elective courses can be selected or rejected more wisely when a prospective student can view videotapes of classes in which students are actually engaged in activities representative of the course.

3. *Vocational counseling:* Chapter 8, "Considering Careers in Television," can be used in its entirety for career education. The chapter also contains references to other materials that may be ordered to supplement this textbook.

Language Arts

The teacher of language arts will find many of the learning experiences listed in the first six chapters in *Television Production Today!* appropriate for the objectives of courses in this area. Some particularly suitable activities might include these:

1. Chapter 1, "Viewing the Message"; Videolab exercises on critical viewing.

2. Chapter 4, "Sounding the Message"; Videolab exercises on selecting music and sound effects for radio shows or commercials.

3. Chapter 5, "Verbalizing the Message"; Videolab exercise 8 on scripting a short story.

Other activities will come to mind as the instructor becomes more aware of the potential of the medium. A writing assignment can encourage unusual creativity when a videotape is played with the sound turned off and students are challenged to write an appropriate script for what they see. Book reports become exciting experiences when complemented by suitable visuals and musical background.

The teacher of language arts will also find most helpful the material on regulation of copyrighted material in Chapter 5, pages 176–178.

Music

Like the teacher of language arts, the teacher of music will find the material on clearance of copyrighted material in the same chapter, most helpful when band, orchestra, and choral groups perform on radio or television.

Additional aids for the teacher of music include the section on acoustics, Chapter 4, pages 118–120, and the brief section on auditions in Chapter 7, pages 275–276. Tight close-ups of a vocalist can be videotaped and played back to enable him or her to follow and analyze breath control habits and to correct flaws in phrasing. One teacher of music appreciation used the technique of supering the name of the musical instrument being featured in an orchestral arrangement to call attention to that instrument without interrupting the music. Another teacher used tight close-up shots of a hand-built organ to explain its intricate parts to a large group of students who otherwise could not have seen the parts clearly enough to identify them.

Even a cursory survey of the music on television will establish its significance in this sound and sight medium.

Physical Education

Just as the music teacher cannot ignore the audio elements in television production, the physical education teacher cannot ignore what the visual elements can contribute to the instructional program. Demonstration of skills in traditionally large classes can be enhanced and improved by the capacity of the television camera to magnify things such as the hand grip for the golf putter, the grip of a baseball bat, the foul shot in basketball, the serve in tennis, or the release of the arrow in archery.

Numerous sports activities are represented in the learning experiences in *Television Production Today!* Videolab activities 1, 2, 3 and 4 in Chapter 2, pages 45–46 involve sportscasting. Play-by-play recording activities appear on pages 135–136 of Chapter 4. Emceeing a sports show is practiced in Videolab exercise 3 on pages 244–245 of Chapter 5. The use of videotape as a teaching tool for swimming and basketball is discussed in Chapter 7 on page 275. No physical education teacher will need to point out the close relationship between sports and television, at least not as long as telecasts of the World Series, the Super Bowl, and the Olympics continue to draw high ratings.

Science

The classroom science teacher can use the television camera for many different purposes. How to dissect a frog and what a microscopic slide reveals are more easily understood when students can see the demonstration magnified many times by the lens of the television camera. The arrangement of elements in a chemical compound can be effectively visualized when table tennis balls can be assembled as a graphic before the television camera to represent NH_4 or NH_4OH. The student who has just won honorable mention in the science fair can share the intricacies of a successful project with large classes of students.

Social Studies

Television, with its influence on the mass audience, is an inseparable part of social studies. Numerous activities in *Television Production Today!* might serve as assignments for classes in American problems, civics, history, economics, government and international affairs. Some possible examples include the following:

1. Newscasting, Chapter 5, Videolab exercise 1, page 182.

2. Television Code, Chapter 5, pages 178–180. (Students could do further research on the Code.)

3. Editorial comment, Chapter 4, page 135.

4. Comparing PBS news with network news, Chapter 1, Videolab exercise 5, page 26.

Speech and Theater Arts

Because so many of the objectives of television are inextricably related to the communication skills in speech and theater arts, the activities of both are closely related. Many of the learning experiences in *Television Production Today!* are helpful to the teacher of speech and theater arts.

Speech and theater students might want to use the rating charts for dramatic shows on page 21 in Chapter 1. This section might provide direction for the discussion of plays seen on television and for those seen on the stage.

Another activity useful for the teacher of acting is Videolab exercise 8 on page 47 of Chapter 2. Other classes may want to participate as members of the audience for this learning experience.

The teacher responsible for directing speakers and actors will find many of the activities in *Television Production Today!* performance-oriented. The performers have just as many specialized responsibilities as the technical crews. The performer's use of the microphone is discussed on pages 120–122 of Chapter 4. Information about performance on radio can be found on page 126 of Chapter 4 in the section on communicating by sound alone. A sample radio script on page 145 of this same chapter, can form the basis of many theater activities.

Theater teachers are constantly searching for methods to develop cooperative relationships between the cast and crews of dramatic productions. The talent's responsibilities as delineated on pages 232–233 in Chapter 6, reinforce the principles necessary for successful play production. The director will find valuable information on properties on pages 224–225 of Chapter 6.

The videotape recorder can make the same lesson available to numerous groups. For example, a single introductory lecture on *Hamlet* played on the videotape recorder in various classrooms can be adapted to individual differences by the follow-up activities selected by each teacher to meet the needs of the particular group's abilities and interests.

All Departments

The videotape recorder has added new dimensions to the field of communication and, after all, that is what teaching is all about—communicating with students to bring about desired behaviors, attitudes, and skills.

No instructor can continue to teach the same way after he or she has been exposed to and involved in the television medium. The possibilities for excellence, the opportunities for meaningful evaluation and criticism, the variety of approaches to instruction with immediate feedback—all these are limited only by the imagination of the teacher willing to include television as a colleague in the instructional process. This powerful medium is here to stay.

PART 4
Supplementary Materials

There are many resources available to the television teacher in the planning of the television course. For example, you may want to examine an MSA curriculum guide like *Radio, Television, and Film in the Secondary School*, edited by Deldee M. Herman and Sharon A. Ratliffe (National Textbook Company). Part of the Michigan Speech Association Curriculum Guide series and developed with the collaboration of 150 teachers, this guide includes chapters on media analysis, history of radio, television and film, equipment, the physical plant, materials, radio production, television production, and film production. The bibliography for each chapter and the appendix on preparing a school program for airing on a local station will be especially helpful.

Additional Resources are located at the end of each chapter of the text. The following can also be of assistance to you in locating materials to meet your specific needs.

Publications

These booklets are published by the National Association of Broadcasters:
1) *Free Television: How It Serves America*
2) *Study Guide on Broadcasting*, which includes study questions and selected readings
3) *Advertising Stopped at 10 o'Clock*

The NAEB publishes a Telecommunication Directory, a list of educational television/public television stations, a list of state authorities, a list of public radio stations, and a list of individual members.

National Association of Educational
Broadcasters
1346 Connecticut Ave., NW
Washington, DC 20036

The NEA has a department of audio-visual instruction and a division of instructional television, with numerous publications specifically designed for the classroom teacher.

National Educational Association
1201 Sixteenth St., NW
Washington, DC 20036

This is a non-profit organization which distributes television materials.

National Instructional Television
Box A
Bloomington, IN 47401

This association publishes a wide variety of materials.

Speech Communication Association
5105 Blacklick Rd.
Annandale, VA 22003

This is a weekly magazine directed to those who are in the radio and television field.

Broadcasting Magazine
1735 De Sales St., NW
Washington, DC 20036

The following books are excellent resources for you or your class to use. In addition, there are many new books on videotape production in local bookstores.

Bermingham, Alan, et al, *The Small TV Studio*, Hastings House, 1975.

Bensinger, Charles, *The Video Guide*, Video Information Publications, Santa Fe, NM, 1982.

Buerki, F.A., *Stagecraft for Non-Professionals*, University of Wisconsin Press, 1970.

Cosgrove, Frances, *Scenes for Student Actors,* (several volumes) Samuel French Inc.

Fedler, Fred. *An Introduction to the Mass Media.* Harcourt, Brace, Jovanovich, 1978.

Hall, Mark, *Broadcast Journalism,* Hastings House, 1971.

Hasling, John, *Fundamentals of Radio Broadcasting,* McGraw-Hill, 1980.

Heighton, Elizabeth and Cunningham, Don, *Advertising in the Broadcast Media.* Wadsworth Publishing Co., 1976.

Lewis, Colby, *TV Director/Interpretor,* Hastings House, 1968.

McInnes, James, *Video in Education and Training,* Focal Press, 1980.

Millerson, Gerald, *Video Camera Techniques,* Focal Press, 1983.

Nisbett, Alec, *The Use of Microphones,* Focal Press, 1974.

Pei, Mario, *Weasel Words: Art of Saying What You Don't Mean,* Harper and Row, 1978.

Rosen, Frederic, *Shooting Video,* Focal Press, 1984.

Stephans, Mitchell, *Broadcast News,* Holt, Rhinehart, and Winston, 1980.

Wilkie, Bernard, *Techniques of Special Effects in TV,* Hastings House, 1979.

Zettl, Herbert, *Television Production Handbook,* (fourth edition) Wadsworth Publishing Co., 1984.

Films and Videotapes

The following firm provides excellent videotapes on television production.

Video International Publishers
1001 3rd St., NW
P.O. Box 1219
Great Falls, MT 59403

"Sound Production for Video"

"Producing a Videotape"

"Format Analysis and Writing for Videotape"

"Sets and Locations for Videotape"

"Preparation and Use of Graphics"

"Editing and Special Effects"

"Mobile Videotape Production"

"What's Wrong: Troubleshooting a Video System"

The following film company has many good films and videotapes on television production, some of which are listed below:

Pyramid Films
Box 1048
Santa Monica, CA 90406

"Making of a Live TV Show"

"Television News Reporter"

"Television Land"

"Sixty-Second Spot"

"Basic Television Terms"

"TV Ads: Our Mini Myths"

The following film company has films and videotapes for television, two of which are listed:

Films Incorporated
1144 Wilmette Ave.
Wilmette, IL 60091

"Six Billion $$$ Sell"

"Seconds to Play"

The 3M company has a videotape series available on ¾ U video cassette. The series is called *The Sight and Sound of Videotape Production.* Individual titles include the following:

"Basic Audio Techniques"

"Camera Techniques for Videotape"

"How to Perform on Television"

"How to Produce a Videotape Program"

"Lighting for Videotape Production"

"Portable Videotape Production Techniques"

"A Practical Guide to Sets and Props for Videotape"

"TV Formats"

"Set Up and Care of Videotapes"

Associations and Organizations

Most radio and TV stations belong to this national organization.

National Association of Broadcasters
1771 N St., NW
Washington, DC 20036

This is an association of cable TV companies.

National Cable Television Association
1724 Massachusetts Ave., NW
Washington, DC 20036

This is the headquarters of the TV director's union. They might provide information for students wishing to become directors.

Director's Guild of America (DGA)
7950 Sunset Blvd.
Los Angeles, CA 90046

This is the association for stations that focus on educational programming.

National Association of Educational
Broadcasters
1346 Connecticut Ave., NW
Washington, DC 20036

This is the union for those appearing on air on radio or television.

American Federation of Television and Radio
Artists (AFTRA)
1350 Avenue of the Americas
New York, NY 10019

This is the union for stagehands for television, film, and theatre.

IATSE
1515 Broadway
New York, NY 10036

Using Your Imagination

Unless you are a teacher with an unlimited budget, you will need to look for classroom materials in unlikely places. You may want to have your name on numerous mailing lists or you may have to accept cast-offs from more affluent professional colleagues. In developing your imagination and ingenuity you may also be able to transform nothing into something.

Throughout *Television Production Today!* you will find suggestions labeled "Economy Note." For instance, on page 81 there is an example of a graphic made from the classified section of the daily newspaper; on page 100 there is a crawl or title drum made from an old washing machine wringer; on page 224 are directions for using old wallpaper sample books.

Cardboard cylinders from paper towels and bathroom tissue can be used to coil cables when crews strike the set. Masking tape can be used to label these cable containers with the length of cable or with the name of the instrument for which the cable or extension cord is to be used. Colored mystic tape on these cylinders can be used to color code them for ready identification.

Another source of free materials is the local newspaper or local print shop. The sheets of aluminum used in offset printing are of no further use to the printer but can be transformed by the television teacher, with the help of cooperative students, into light reflection screens or thunder sheets for sound effects. The print shop often has cast-off headline letters, posters, and uneven strips of cardboard useful in preparing graphics.

If you teach in a town with an educational television station, you might ask for their cast-off graphics. Sometimes their discarded signs can be used to illustrate the aspect ratio, coloring, spacing, and effective and ineffective techniques. Title cards that cannot be used a second time by the station can supply you with examples of lettering and mounting of pictures.

Even the local movie theater can provide poster ads to check effectiveness on camera. Many of the small pictures of scenes from the movies are horizontal and measure about 24″ × 18″.

Yet another source of free material is the local department store, which uses a variety of materials for window displays. Old racks, stands, scraps of material, artificial grass, poles, models, styrofoam forms, platters, turntables—their cast-offs— can become a reservoir of properties and graphic supplies that the television camera can transform into respectable images when lighted imaginatively.

The neighborhood construction company might donate a bucket or two of slag, gravel, and sand that can be displayed in a flat tray for tight close-up shots to simulate parks, roadways, and beaches.

The hardware dealer may be willing to donate bits and pieces of wire screen through which a camera lens can be focused for unusual effects or wall shadows. Window shades provide a rough-textured canvas background on which students can paint bookcases, blooming fruit trees, and storm clouds which look like the real thing on camera. The rollers make it easy to raise or lower these simulated backgrounds.

The ice cream store can save for you empty gallon tubs of cardboard, which can be painted to provide pedestals for the display of models, statuary, and similar exhibits. If you have enough of these cylindrical cartons to stack them five or six feet high, they will create a wall background suitable for an awards ceremony with loving cups and trophies displayed on them.

A good teacher is always searching for more effective instructional materials. Nothing takes the place of a generous budget to supply the operational needs, but the ingenuity, creativity, and imagination of both teacher and students can supply many of the needs inherent in a visual medium such as television communication.

PART 5

Learning Experiences

The chapters of *Television Production Today!* include suggestions for student discussion called "Take Two" and opportunities for practical experiences called "Videolabs." These are not intended to be required assignments, but are intended to serve as a guide for students and teachers to use in deciding on activities. The following guidelines should make the experiences and activities meaningful.

1. Students should be aware of the goals and objectives of each activity. Students and teacher should understand in advance what they wish to accomplish. For example, if the student's goal is speed of operation and the instructor's goal is accuracy of lens choice, there may be disagreement when the performance is evaluated. Understanding goals and objectives is also extremely important for those experiences that involve critical evaluation of the medium. For the seemingly simple assignment of watching a television program, students must understand what they are looking for and the criteria they should be using.

Every experience, therefore, should be prefaced by a discussion of "What am I supposed to get out of this? What am I supposed to be learning? How can I tell when I have succeeded? What proof of my achievement will I have?" Upon the completion of an activity, the teacher should assist the student in evaluating his or her achievement by discussing problems such as this: When a crew member fails to respond to my directions with accuracy and dispatch, is it due to my inadequate planning, poor choice of diagrams, imprecise wording, or unreasonable expectations?

2. Supplies and equipment should be available in the classroom or studio before any activities begin. Planning that conserves time is especially important in an industry in which every minute of time is an expensive item. Both the students' and the teacher's plans should include a "check in advance" list to avoid disrupting an activity.

3. Students should operate as if they were in a real television studio. They should understand the importance of procedures, the standards of excellence, and the necessary set of values. The television classroom or studio should conform as nearly as possible to the demands of an actual broadcast. The self-discipline demanded of crew members as part of the production team is more than a by-product of television activities; it is a major consideration.

4. *The role of the teacher* in a television course cannot be underestimated. Few classroom activities offer a better opportunity for the teacher to become a member of the team and to participate as a guide while students explore the learning experiences. The television production teacher guides, leads, and directs; the television production teacher serves as a resource consultant, providing aids and resources not otherwise available to the students; the television production teacher shares with students the evaluation of both the process and the product of the learning activities suggested in *Television Production Today!*

5. Wherever possible, allow the students to present their programs to other students. Television programs are meant to be viewed. When students know that their program will be viewed by their peers, they will put extra effort and pride in their work. If programs are recorded and then forgotten, students have no motivation to do well. Perhaps "Emmy" trophies can be awarded as a culminating activity, with students voting for outstanding performances.

Assignments and Activities

Students will understand and retain the ideas contained in the text if these concepts are incorporated into class activities. If the student can see how each idea is used in a production, the concept will be viewed as a tool to be used in the production. In addition, it will help students appreciate what they see on TV since they have attempted to create in their studios what is done in the larger commercial studios. Only after a student has tried to direct a television newscast can he or she clearly understand and appreciate what goes into the local 11 PM newscast on the local station.

All of the class activities in *Television Production Today!* and in this *Book* can be modified to meet the needs of your local studio. Allow students time to develop the idea, write a script, produce, and tape each activity or assignment.

I have found it helpful to present assignments in writing, including due dates and the blank script forms that are going to be needed. You might examine the TV commercial, TV drama, and TV newscast assignments in this *Book,* and you are welcome to use these as hand outs. In this way if a student were absent he or she could use the assignment sheet to review the concepts expected. Often, when I studied geometry, I understood what the instructor said as he explained it, but when I got home, with no examples, the concepts were foreign to me. Perhaps I was unique in this, but I think not. Many of the script forms found in the text or the sample scripts in this teacher's *Book* will help.

For many of the assignments, it is a good idea to give a complete packet of materials to each student or team. For example, for the One-Minute TV Commercial Assignment, provide students with a blank Studio Fax Sheet (a sheet listing the equipment and crew needed to produce the project), a blank Video Script Form, and a blank Floor Plan. Have them complete the worksheets before attempting to use the studio for the production. There are other forms in this *Book* that you may want to include in an assignment. The masters for these forms appear on pages 21–35. They can be removed for easy photocopying. Grade the student on each part. Grades on the One-Minute TV Commercial, for example, can be given on 1) the written script; 2) the floor plan; and 3) the final production.

In addition, it would be beneficial for each student to provide a "treatment" for each production. A treatment is a short description of what is to be accomplished in the commercial or program. It is easier to have a student redirect his or her own thinking before writing a complete script for a program that will go nowhere. After you have approved their projects, students can then complete the scripts, floor plans, etc.

In addition to the assignments provided here, there are many class activities provided for the students in *Television Production Today!* In fact, if yours is a one-semester course, it will be necessary to determine which assignments will be most useful, as time will limit what you can cover. It is *important,* however, to use the classroom activities. *Television Production Today!* is designed to provide a total learning experience that includes class activities. Don't be afraid to adapt any of these assignments to fit your needs. It is sometimes necessary to alter assignments depending on the character of the class itself. In addition, use your own assignments and activities to individualize the text for your needs.

Many of the scripts and assignments may be used as they appear in the text. For example, students may produce the radio drama as it is presented in the text. It is a simple drama that can be easily produced by a class with minimal equipment. Music and sound effects can easily be found for this production. Since it is "public domain," it can be used on any radio station with no worry on royalties.

I hope you find these assignments to be helpful for your needs. They are the heart of any production course.

The following assignments can be used as class exercises. These can be produced on simple radio and television equipment. Most production classes have the equipment necessary. You can modify the assignments to suit the needs of your studio and situation.

Chapter 1 Viewing the Message

1. Ask students to interview each other on the second day of class. Have them pretend that they are hosting a local radio talk show and they are interviewing a guest. Have students plan an *exact* three-minute interview. Emphasize to them that exact timing is important. Advise them to use a stop watch.

Encourage creativity. Ask students what it takes to make a radio interview interesting and have them incorporate their ideas in the project. Record the interviews and play them back to the class. Start a teacher-directed class discussion and have the students critique each one.

If you wish, hold on to this first project until you near the end of the course. Play the interviews back along with interviews they produced later in the course. Have the students critique both of their interviews. Ask students to discuss the difference between them.

2. Moment in broadcast history. Assign each student to pick an event or person that had an effect on the history of broadcasting. It could be a modern broadcaster or an earlier figure, such as Edward R. Murrow. Have the students produce their radio assignments using music or sound effects. If they sound professional, why not submit them to your local radio station or cable TV's alpha numeric channel for airing?

Chapter 2   Assessing the Medium

1. Any of the Videolab exercises would make good projects for students to produce.

2. A good way to show the difference between radio and television is to assign the class to create commercials for a product. Have the students work in groups of two. Choose one product for the whole class to use for each medium. This is a good way to show students the different approaches to creating a commercial. Both commercial spots should be about 30 to 60 seconds long. The radio spot should focus on the listener's imagination. The television commercial should emphasize the visual elements.

Once their ad commercials are complete, have students present their projects to the class. Encourage creativity. If the students wish, they can bring some visuals they plan to use or act out the parts.

The students do not have to write out complete scripts because this will be taught in a later chapter.

Chapter 3   Visualizing the Message

1. Video collage. Have the students pick a modern song that has lyrics that are easily understood and have a message. Because some of the lyrics used in contemporary songs may be questionable for use, you may have to supervise the students. The students should prepare a video script including every line of the song used. They should obtain pictures or slides representing each line or idea of the song. The student should decide if he or she should cut or dissolve to each visual used.

On the day of production, the student should bring in all visuals carefully mounted and numbered and divided according to the camera used. In addition, a video cassette or recording must be brought in. Have students provide you with a copy of the script and a copy of the floor plan to be used during production. (See Sample Forms and Handouts beginning on page 19.) Make up a rotation sheet allowing students to

serve as crew for the production. Each student directs his or her own production.

Because this project may take as much as one class period to rehearse and record, you might wish to break the class into groups of two for its production.

2. Television commercial. Use the handout on page 21 for this activity.

3. Have the students produce a three-minute talk demonstration as assigned in the Videolab text. They should work in groups of two. One will serve as host, the other will direct. Have students submit a complete script and a floor plan. The program should be recorded on videotape.

Chapter 4   Sounding the Message

1. Straight radio commercial. Assign the students to write a one-minute straight radio commercial about a product or service (approximately 125 words). The students can use the sample script on page 137 of the text as their guide. The script should have a motive appeal (savings, health, and so on). The students may need your help in this area. Once they have submitted a written script, have them produce their project. Stress the importance of voice, pronunciation, ease in reading, and believability. Record the commercials and play them back to the class. Have the students critique each one.

2. Production commercial. Have the students take the same product or service they used above and write a commercial that includes music in the beginning, end, or throughout the commercial. Stress the importance of music to create mood. Perhaps a sound effect can be used. The example in the text on page 139 can be used as a guide. Record and play these back to the class.

3. Situation radio commercial. Have the students work singly or in groups of two to write a situation commercial involving actors, music, and sound effects. Use the text's example on page 140 of this chapter as a guide. Have the students submit a script. This is a project that can involve the whole class in producing the commercials.

4. Produce a radio drama. Have the class produce the radio drama on page 145 of the text. If you wish, you can have students create their own radio drama. Have students select one or two and produce it for radio.

5. Use some of the assignments in *Television Production Today!* under the Videolab section. You can adapt the suggestions of this chapter to suit your needs.

Chapter 5   Verbalizing the Message

1. Use the Videolab exercises in this chapter of *Television Production Today!* as suggested assignments for your class.

2. Newsbreak assignment. This is a good project for students to produce as a beginning exercise. Have them read the newsbreak script provided in the text on page 168. Then have students create a news story using the sample script as a guide. The scripts and programs should include the following: 1) an opening and closing, using logos and music; 2) a booth announcer's opening and closing; 3) a key of the name (if your equipment can do this); and 4) at least two pictures of the stories pulled from newspapers or magazines (the pictures should be mounted). The anchor should write the script. One copy should be given to the director. The anchor should keep the other.

The students will produce this exercise in a round robin. Make a rotation chart allowing every student to rotate through every job in the studio.

3. Write a short TV script for a one-minute Public Service Announcement. Be sure to include all the necessary audio and video elements to make this a successful production. Be sure to write in the necessary information to tell the director and camera operator what shots are required. Record these on videotape and play back for analysis. These can be produced in studios with two or three cameras. Adapt the script as necessary. This assignment can also be produced in a classroom on a single camera system if necessary.

4. TV drama. Use the handout on page 23 for this assignment. Divide the class into groups of three or four. Have each group pick a short scene from a play that can be adapted for television. The scene should last approximately four to five minutes. Each group will divide themselves into actors and a director. They should 1) cut the selection; 2) create a floor plan; 3) block the action; 4) memorize the dialogue; 5) light the scene; 6) secure a simple set; and 7) produce the scene. Let the rest of the class serve as crew.

Chapter 6   Producing the Message

1. A 15-minute newscast. This can be a final project for the school year. The class will have the opportunity to produce a newscast. Use the handout on page 25 as your guide. The class can adapt it any way to suit its needs.

2. Any of the Videolab exercises for this chapter would make good projects for students to produce.

Chapter 7   Taping the Message

1. Try an exercise on editing an audio tape. First teach students how to splice audio tape with a splicing block and a splicing tape. Then, using an audio tape recorder, have students count slowly from one to 10. Tell them to edit out all the even numbers so that they hear only the odd numbers (1-3-5-7-9). Students may need your help for this exercise.

2. To teach students how to insert edit, have them first do a video project. This project can be anything. For example one student can cover a marathon race. The student may interview some of the runners taking part in the race, shoot some wild videos of the runners winding their way around the town, and then do an interview with the winner. In the editing room, show students how to insert a sequence to another part of the tape. For example, you can insert a wild video between one of the interviews.

3. Take the students to a local cable company studio for practice on a VHS editing deck. Perhaps your school's audio/visual director can demonstrate editing techniques on the school's VHS decks.

4. Have the students complete the exercises in the Videolab section of this chapter in *Television Production Today!*

Chapter 8   Considering Careers in Television

1. In a large television station, more than 100 people may be responsible for the 11 PM newscast. Most people only see the on-air performers who deliver the news, not the people behind the scenes—those who help put the newscast together.

Watch a typical newscast and look at the credits at the end of the program. Have the students pick a job that interests them and present a paper about it. This paper should include what the job is, a description, qualifications for this type of position, and what type of person they think would be happy in this job (a camera engineer, for example, likes working with her hands and likes fixing cameras). A good way to do this project is to interview someone who holds this position.

The paper should be four pages long, double-spaced, typed.

PART 6

Sample Forms and Handouts

This section contains materials that have been designed for easy copying so that you can use them for student handouts. They include both activity materials and sample forms that can be adapted to a great variety of projects:

One-Minute TV Commercial
TV Drama Assignment
TV Newscast Assignment
Studio Floor Plan form
Studio Fax Sheet form
Storyboard Outline form
Storyboard Script form
Video Script form
Crossword Puzzles

Name: _____ **Date:** _____

One-Minute TV Commercial

We have seen how advertising agencies utilize motive appeals to sell a product or service. We have seen also that the NAB suggests establishing the motive appeal, proving the motive appeal, and urging the audience to action.

The basic motives apply to television as well as radio and newspaper advertising. The major difference, however, is that the presentation must be visual for TV. The straight commercial often heard on radio would be extremely dull seen on TV. The audience expects to see the product or a demonstration of the product on the screen. Therefore just showing a person talking about the product is a poor example of how to create a TV commercial.

Often more creativity has gone into a one-minute TV commercial than the program it is sponsoring.

There are many types of TV commercials seen on TV. Among them:

- Situational or dramatic: This is where a one-minute drama is presented. This would include writing dialogue, designing a simple set, choosing a cast, memorizing parts, and taping a one-minute drama about the product.

- Real people commercials: This involves interviewing "real people" to explain the great uses of the product or service.

- Demonstration: This is where a salesperson or announcer demonstrates the virtues of a product. This is more than just a straight commercial. It utilizes the sight element of TV.

Assignment for a TV Commercial

You are to write, produce, and direct a one-minute commercial for TV. I hope you will utilize *all* of the elements we have studied so far to create the best TV production possible. You are to assume a sponsor has come to you, a producer/director of a TV station, and wants to advertise on your station. The sponsor leaves it up to you to create the commercial. It is your job to sell the sponsor's product during a one-minute spot, which will be shown during the "Tonight Show" at 11 PM in three weeks.

For this assignment you must do the following:

- Write a one-minute TV commercial.

- Make a floor plan indicating where cameras and lights should be placed.

- Design a simple set with furniture if needed.

- Provide a camera plot for *each* camera to be used.

- Work with the talent to get what you may need. Be sure to have the script early so that the talent has time to memorize it. You may ask anyone in the class to serve as talent for you.

On the following page you will find suggestions and steps to help you in this assignment.

Name: _____ Date: _____

Suggestions for Creating a TV Commercial

1. Pick a real product, one that could be shown on TV.

2. Make the commercial original. Do not merely rewrite an idea we have already seen on TV. This should be your own idea.

3. Pick the motive appeal you are going to establish. Make it only one appeal and make it simple.

4. Have the elements in the commercial establish the motive appeal you have chosen.

5. Make the commercial a dramatization, demonstration, or interview with "real people." Pick the one which best suits your product.

6. Make any graphics that will be used to visualize the product. Make graphics with press-on letters, letter-on, or other suitable device. Hand-lettered graphics will not be acceptable.

7. Don't forget the logo. This may be the product or a graphic of the product.

8. Decide on what kind of a set should be used. You can get props from the large prop room, club rooms, etc. If the things you need are not available in school, you must furnish them.

9. Make a camera and lighting plot.

10. You should have at least two copies of the script.

11. Pick a cast and give them a copy of the script early enough so they may memorize lines. You may even bring in outside talent providing they are free to come to the studio during your class period.

12. You will have one class period to rehearse, set up, light, and make a tape of this commercial.

13. Be sure to give each camera operator a shot chart so he or she can get to the next shot quickly.

Make this the best effort you have done. Use all of the elements of TV discussed in this text. Use lights, graphics, and TV directing to make this an outstanding assignment. This is exactly what a TV director must do. You have been given all the elements; now it is up to you as a director to take a product or service and present it in such a way that it will be appealing for the TV audience.

Now you know why the directors are paid well.

GOOD LUCK!

Name: _____ **Date:** _____

TV Drama Assignment

Up to now we have concentrated on single impressions on the screen, use of cuts, dissolves, lighting, and so on. This exercise is designed to give you a chance to use these principles in a drama situation. You will also see the added dimension of video over that of radio drama produced earlier.

Principles

1. Conform your shots to the meaning of the script.

2. To interpret the program well, you must understand all the meanings of characterization and how they interpret the situation.

3. Recognize all the individual picture ideas and where they change at any given moment.

4. Reinforce these changes in the mood or content in the program by definite visual changes:

- A performer can sit or rise and walk to a new place.
- Camera changes can be made—a 2-shot if both characters are important—a CU if necessary.

5. The rate of cutting should follow the mood and tempo of the selection.

6. Use high or low camera angles.

7. Use high or low key lighting.

8. Make each character dominant by use of the following:

- Use a CU of the character.
- Have the character face the camera while others face away.
- Have the character closer to the camera.
- Have the character sitting while others stand, or have the character stand while others sit.
- Have the character move while others stand still.

9. Provide a script for everyone in the cast and the director.

10. Go over each line of the cutting and determine camera angles and changes.

11. The director should help to block the scene and help with characterizations.

12. Keep a cover shot for any unanticipated movement.

Name: _____ Date: _____

Do the Following to Complete the Assignment

1. Pick a scene from a play of about four to five minutes with at least two characters.

2. Secure a simple set of furniture, props, and costumes.

3. Prepare a complete script.

4. Prepare a complete floor plan including:

   - set

   - furniture

   - characters and movements

   - mike placement

   - lighting

It is hoped this assignment will give you a real experience in using television as a means of communicating. It can be a very creative experience if you will use this opportunity to develop yourself as a producer/director/performer.

GOOD LUCK!

Name: _____ Date: _____

TV Newscast Assignment

This exercise will consists of a 15-minute, TV newscast-sports-weather-editorial program. The production team will divide themselves into reporters, anchor person(s), weather forcaster, editorial director, and director. Videotape inserts can be used for your stories.

Format

The show can be broken generally into the following:

OPEN	:30
NEWS	3:00
INTERVIEW	2:30
COMMERCIAL	1:00
NEWS	1:00
WEATHER	2:00
SPORTS	2:00
COMMERCIAL	1:00
EDITORIAL	1:30
CLOSING	:30
TOTAL	15:00

Make this newscast as visual as possible. The following visual elements may be used: 1) live news, 2) videotape, 3) pictures mounted on tag board, 4) keys, 5) film shot with a voice over, 6) weather maps and dials made up, 7) scores and supers made over slides of sports scenes, and 8) opening and closing logos.

News

Prepare each story to be as visual as possible. A videotape remote will help in the presentation of the story. Use reporters and videotape as much as possible. Pictures should be used where possible.

Interview

Prepare a live interview to be used in the newscast. The interviewer will decide who to interview, prepare a list of questions, make sure the person being interviewed is in the studio when needed, and conduct the interview.

Weather

The weather person will prepare his or her own weather forecast and design a set and graphics needed for the weather. Prepare some weather dials, and make it visual.

Name: _____ **Date:** _____

Sports

The sports reporter should prepare about two minutes of sports and prepare all visuals necessary to show scores and so on.

Editorial

An editorial representing the views of the station's management shall be presented on camera.

Director

The director shall produce a floor plan of the entire newscast (with the help of the entire team) and direct the live production and taped inserts. Lighting is important as well as audio, including music and mike placement.

Helpful Hints

- Each story should be visual (one PIX or tape coverage).
- Each story should be carefully timed.
- All videotapes should be shot and edited for airing in the newscast.
- Commercials may be live or on tape.
- Shot charts should be prepared for the camera operators.
- A complete script should be created for the entire show.
- The entire production should be front timed to make sure it fits into 15 minutes. Each sequence (interview, etc.) should be back timed to make sure they are finished in time for next sequence.

GOOD LUCK!

STUDIO FAX SHEET

Program: Period: Facilities Needed for: Date: ☐ Rehearsal ☐ Taping ☐ Editing/Dubs	Production Team:	Job:

Studio Audio Equipment
(check equipment needed)

☐ Audio Console
☐ Cart/Rec Player
☐ Cart Player Only
☐ Cassette Recorder
☐ R/R Recorder
☐ Console Mike
☐ Floor Mike
☐ Mini-Boom Mike
☐ Desk Mike
☐ Lavaliere Mike
☐ Blank Cassette Tape
☐ Blank R/R Tape
☐ _____

Studio Video Equipment
(check equipment needed)

☐ Studio Color Cameras
☐ Color Video S.E.G.
☐ EIAJ Recorder
☐ VHS Recorder
☐ U-matic Recorder
☐ Large Menu Board
☐ Small Menu Board
☐ O'head Projector
☐ Opaque Projector
☐ 8 mm Projector
☐ 16 mm Projector
☐ Music/Graphic Stand
☐ Blank EIAJ Tape
☐ Blank VHS Tape
☐ Blank U-matic Tape
☐ _____
☐ Scenery (specify)

Crew

_____ Producer	_____ Director
_____ Assistant Director	_____ Camera Operators
_____ Camera Operators	_____ Camera Operators
_____ Technical Director	_____ Floor Manager
_____ Light Director	_____ Production Assistant
_____ Audio Technician	_____ Booth Announcer/Talent(s)
_____ VTR Operator	

Software Titles

Audio Tapes	Slides
_____	_____
_____	_____
Video Tapes	Graphics
_____	_____
_____	_____

STUDIO FLOOR PLAN

Project:		Page ☐ of ☐
Producers:	**Talent:**	

control room
window

door

STORYBOARD OUTLINE

a

b

c

d

e

f

g

h

i

j

k

l

STORYBOARD SCRIPT

Project:	Page ☐ of ☐
Producers:	Presentation:

VIDEO	AUDIO

Name: _____ **Date:** _____

VIDEO SCRIPT FORM

Project: _____ **Page:** _____

Producer(s): _____

DIRECTOR	VIDEO	AUDIO

Crossword Puzzles

Here you will find one crossword puzzle for each chapter of the text. You may want to use them instead of the quizzes for these chapters, or use them as extra credit items. The solutions to the crossword puzzles appear on page 75.

Crossword puzzles can be fun for your students. These were created easily on an Apple computer using *Cross Word Magic* by L & S Software. This is an inexpensive program that can be used to create almost instant crossword puzzles.

Chapter 1 Crossword Puzzle

Across Clues

4. WTBS and WGN are examples of a
_____.

7. The first radio network to broadcast a
coast to coast radio program.

8. The first radio station on the air with a
regular broadcast schedule.

9. A method of providing programs to
homes by the use of small dishes on roofs of
homes (abbreviation).

10. Abbreviation of the federal regulatory
group governing broadcast stations.

11. The largest company providing ratings
to broadcast stations is A.C. _____.

12. The time period in broadcast schedules
from 7 PM to 11 PM is known as
_____ time.

Down Clues

1. Another term for commercials is
_____.

2. The name of the magazine read by most
people in the broadcasting profession.

3. Another word used to eliminate commercials by fast forwarding a video recorder.

5. Broadcasters agree to operate in public
interest, convenience, and _____.

6. Both sides of controversial issues are to
be aired according to the _____
Doctrine.

Chapter 2   Crossword Puzzle

Across Clues

2. Recorded laugh tracks are referred to as _____ laughter.

5. This medium is referred to as "theatre of the mind."

6. Three elements are necessary for communication. A sender, a message, and a

_____.

8. Broadcast band now broadcasting mainly news and talk shows.

Down Clues

1. Interpreting ideas by using your own experience and feeling help to _____ the message.

2. A process of inserting a person or scene by the use of a green screen is called _____ key.

3. A sponsor of one of Dick Orkin's radio commercials.

4. The text compares TV with what other art form in delivering a message?

7. Using videotape to replace film in news is often called _____.

9. The trucks used by news crews to broadcast live stories on TV.

Chapter 3   Crossword Puzzle

Across Clues

4. Most popular spotlight in TV lighting.

5. A telephoto lens produces a _____ depth of field.

7. The best camera pickup tube for non-broadcast cameras under low lighting conditions.

9. To move the camera up and down.

10. TV directors go to this shot when they do not know what will be coming next.

11. Two cameras are on the air at the same time.

12. A type of TV lens allowing for close-ups and far away shots without moving the camera.

Down Clues

1. A type of shot in television where the camera becomes a character.

2. One camera slowly comes on the air while the other camera slowly goes off the air.

3. The main light used on a set.

6. In order for the camera operator to get proper color, he or she must _____ balance.

8. Lateral movement of the camera and dolly to the left or right.

10. The fast way of changing from one camera to another.

11. A flood light producing light eliminating some shadows on the set.

Chapter 4   Crossword Puzzle

Across Clues

1. Term for cartridge used to play music or commercials.

2. If the sound is too low, the announcer is said to be "in the _____."

3. When an audio engineer watches the VU meter to check levels, he or she is said to "ride _____."

4. One must _____ a record to make sure it will start exactly on time and at the right spot.

7. A type of microphone used for remote outdoor broadcasts.

8. The name of the mixer used for combining mikes and turntables.

10. Type of microphone used for music also called a velocity mike.

Down Clues

1. Type of microphone with a heart-shaped pickup pattern.

2. Radio can broadcast only three elements: the voice, sound effects, and _____.

5. Pickup pattern from a microphone with only one live side.

6. A type of microphone usually worn around the neck.

9. A short term for potentiometer on an audio board.

Chapter 5   Crossword Puzzle

Across Clues

5. TV standards eliminating profanity and other possible problems are found in the NAB_____.

6. Starting a TV program without credits is often referred to as a _____opening.

7. You must obtain permission when using published works to avoid problems with _____.

10. A variation of a TV script using drawings and pictures is called a _____ board.

12. A type of TV program using a fully scripted format.

Down Clues

1. The 3 × 4 TV screen is referred to as _____ ratio.

2. The TV script giving the time from the beginning to the end is called _____ timing.

3. The TV script is usually divided into two columns—the audio and the _____.

4. The major organization holding musical copyrights to be paid by radio and TV stations.

8. A script term for the word "picture."

9. A time of show utilizing a partially scripted format.

11. The script term for medium shot used by a director.

Chapter 6   Crossword Puzzle

Across Clues

1. The light on the camera that indicates it is on the air is called a _____ light.

4. The person who is an extension of the director in the studio is called a _____ manager.

6. The person responsible for microphones and sound effects is the _____ technician.

7. In order to get the correct colors, the camera operator must _____ balance the camera.

9. The person in charge of the telecast is the _____.

12. The technical director is often referred to as a _____.

13. The count down in an introduction of a film or commercial is called a _____ cue.

Down Clues

2. The f stop on a camera is another term for the _____.

3. Camera operators use a _____ chart for complicated TV programs.

5. The audio man must often _____ gain on mikes.

8. An easel-like stand used to hold graphics is often called a _____.

10. On-camera performers are often referred to as _____.

11. People or objects shot by themselves with no scenery are called shots in _____.

Chapter 7   Crossword Puzzle

Across Clues

3. A type of edit whereby new material is edited into the middle of a sequence.

6. Videotape recorders use two video _____ located on a bar which spins at a high speed.

7. A type of edit used to piece together different parts of the program from different locations.

10. A TV camera with a built-in video recorder.

Down Clues

1. _____ video is the term used when the camera operator shoots extra video to be inserted later.

2. A type of edit when one uses the pause button on a recorder to edit videotape.

4. A term used to show the reporter with the person being interviewed. This is shot after the interview is over.

5. A term used when a reporter stands in front of a building used for a story as an intro.

8. Term for the space in front of someone's face as he or she faces right or left on the TV screen.

9. Term used for the space between the top of a performer's head and the top of the TV screen.

PART 7

Evaluation and Assessment

Television Production Today! poses questions that guide students to determining for themselves the amount of knowledge and skills that they are acquiring. It also encourages students to think about their developing critical appreciation skills. As a teacher, you will see evidence of achievement and student response to the behavioral objectives that you have established for your course.

In addition you will probably feel the need for written tests to measure student progress. This section includes a test for each chapter of *Television Production Today!*

Included in this part is a Performance Evaluation form. It can easily be copied and used as a hand out. It can be used to encourage thoughtful consideration of both the preparation and the presentation of a TV production.

Name: _____ Date: _____

Performance Evaluation

Preparation

Yes No

☐ ☐ **1.** Did the performance look as if the student had spent enough time and effort in preparation?

☐ ☐ **2.** Did the student have a legible rundown sheet for the camera operator?

☐ ☐ **3.** Did the order of events show advance planning?

☐ ☐ **4.** Was the student sufficiently familiar with the content to avoid hesitation and uncertainty?

☐ ☐ **5.** Were the graphics carefully and correctly prepared?

☐ ☐ **6.** Did the student check in rehearsal those items requiring a check?

☐ ☐ **7.** Did the student prepare an accurate floor plan?

☐ ☐ **8.** Was the script sufficient for all members of talent and crew to perform successfully?

☐ ☐ **9.** Did all personnel act as members of a team?

Presentation

Yes No

☐ ☐ **1.** Did the talent follow correct studio procedure by responding to cues from the floor manager?

☐ ☐ **2.** Did the talent follow the rules of good speech by speaking distinctly, with adequate volume, and in a conversational tone?

☐ ☐ **3.** Was there good eye contact with the audience (in this case, the camera lens)?

☐ ☐ **4.** Were visuals used effectively to take advantage of the television medium?

☐ ☐ **5.** Did the presentation meet the time limits?

☐ ☐ **6.** Was use of the script obvious?

☐ ☐ **7.** Was the presentation visual in nature?

☐ ☐ **8.** Did the talent communicate on a one-to-one basis?

☐ ☐ **9.** Did the presentation follow an organized progression?

☐ ☐ **10.** Did the choice of music enhance the mood of the performance?

Chapter Tests

It's a good idea to provide a short test at the end of each chapter. These tests increase the student's level of concern as he or she reads an assigned chapter in *Television Production Today!* If a student knows a short test will be given at the end of each chapter reading, he or she, in all probability, will take a more careful look at the readings.

The tests have 10 questions for each chapter. If you wish, you can include additional questions of your own to supplement the readings in the text. An essay question is included in each chapter test. You may want to give students extra time to answer this part of the test, or use the essay as a take-home assignment.

To help the students prepare for the tests, start a teacher-directed class discussion at the end of each chapter reading. Review the main points and discuss key terms.

For your convenience, the tests can be pulled from this *Book* for easy photocopying.

Name: _____ **Date:** _____

Chapter 1   Viewing the Message

1. Name two companies that provide ratings information to radio and TV stations.

_____

_____

2. The FCC has recently changed the number of radio and TV stations one individual or group may own. How many radio or TV stations could you own?

_____

3. What radio station is considered to be the first licensed radio station in the United States? Is the station still on the air?

_____

4. List two items that might be considered "soft news" in a radio or TV news broadcast.

_____

_____

5. Why are some TV stations dubbed "superstations"? What are the call letters of one such station?

_____

_____

_____

6. What is the difference between local origination programs and "public access programs"?

_____

_____

_____

7. Name two emotional appeals advertisers use to sell their products on television and radio. List at least one example for each of the appeals.

_____

_____

8. What is the name of the trade magazine most read by people in the broadcast industry?

_____

Name: _____ **Date:** _____

9. Why are advertisers and broadcast stations concerned with the growth of video recorders in the homes?

_____

_____

10. People react critically to TV programs in different ways. Give two reasons why two different people might react differently to the same TV program.

_____

_____

Essay Question

(Use a separate sheet of paper for your response.)

The growth of video technology has affected TV viewing. The emergence of VCRs, laser discs, and video recorders and the expansion of cable TV has given viewers more choices in viewing programs. Do you see these changes as good or bad? Explain why. How do you think television will affect the future?

Chapter 2   Assessing the Medium

1. Why do some advertisers prefer to advertise on radio rather than television or newspapers?

_____

_____

_____

2. Performing on television is different from performing on the stage. Present at least two differences between performing in front of a TV camera and performing on the stage.

_____

_____

_____

_____

3. Why is "chroma key" so valuable for a TV news broadcast?

_____

_____

_____

4. Why is radio often referred to as "theatre of the mind"?

_____

_____

_____

_____

5. Why do most news stations now use videotape to record their stories rather than film?

_____

_____

_____

6. What makes FM radio ideal for broadcasting music?

_____

_____

7. Radio can make use of only three elements for creating a program. One, of course, is the actor's voice and words; another is music. What is the third element that can be used during a radio broadcast?

_____

Name: _____ Date: _____

8. Most minicams used for remote TV coverage are often referred to as "ENG" cameras. What does the acronym ENG stand for?

_____

9. Radio allows an announcer to speak to thousands of people at the same time. However, how many people should the announcer think he or she is talking to? Why?

_____

_____

_____

_____

10. There are three parts to an effective communication model. Name the three parts.

_____

_____

_____

Essay Question

(Use a separate sheet of paper for your response.)

Pick an imaginary product that could be sold on radio and television and think of an ad commercial for each medium. How will the radio ad commercial differ from the one directed for television? In your opinion, which is more effective in sending your message across? Explain your answer.

Chapter 3   Visualizing the Message

1. Name at least two types of pickup tubes used in a television camera. Name the advantages and disadvantages for each one.

_____

_____

_____

2. Explain the difference between depth of focus and depth of field.

_____

_____

_____

3. As a director, what term or terms would one use to instruct a camera operator to do each of the following?

a. Move the camera and dolly to the right to follow swimmers in a meet.

_____

b. Move the camera in a semi-circle to the left to go from a profile shot of a pianist to a close-up of his or her hands.

_____

c. Move the camera straight back from the talent.

_____

d. After starting with a close-up of someone's boots, the camera slowly comes up to a shot of the person's face.

_____

e. Move the camera (not the tripod) to the left to pick up the next speaker in a discussion.

_____

4. To make the talent appear insignificant or unimportant, would the director use a high angle or low angle shot?

_____

5. A producer is sent with a camera crew to cover a story about the crowded expressways during rush hour. Should the producer tell the camera operator to use a wide angle or telephoto lens to show the expressway? Why?

_____

_____

_____

Name: _____ **Date:** _____

6. Explain the difference between an objective and a subjective camera shot.

_____

_____

_____

_____

7. Why is a floor plan necessary to plan any TV production? What should be included in any standard floor plan?

_____

_____

_____

_____

8. Three point lighting consists of three types of lights on a TV set. List the three types of lighting.

_____

_____

_____

9. Television is a two dimensional medium (height and width). However, a TV director has several tricks which can simulate three dimensions. List three ways a director can create dimensions in his or her shots.

_____

_____

_____

10. It is important to remember that all graphics are to be created in aspect ratio. What is the television screen's aspect ratio?

_____

Essay Question

(Use a separate sheet of paper for your response.)

You have been asked to direct a one-minute television commercial for a raspberry-flavored soft drink. Knowing that visuals are important in communicating the message, what visuals would you use to sell this soft drink? Explain your answer.

Chapter 4   Sounding the Message

1. Briefly describe the pickup pattern of the following microphones used in broadcasting.

   a. unidirectional

   _____

   _____

   b. bidirectional

   _____

   _____

   c. omnidirectional

   _____

   _____

   d. cardioid

   _____

   _____

2. Name the type of microphone (not pickup pattern) that would best suit each situation below and briefly tell why.

   a. used outdoors during a football game

   _____

   b. used as a lavaliere mike for news anchors

   _____

   c. used in the middle of a table to pick up many people sitting around the table for a discussion

   _____

3. Define the following audio terms:

   a. board

   _____

   b. pot

   _____

   c. cart

   _____

   d. VU meter

   _____

Name: _____ Date: _____

4. Why is it a good idea to include gestures and facial expressions on radio even though no one may see the talent?

_____

_____

5.   a. What term is used if the announcer is not loud enough and the VU meter is low?

_____

   b. What term is used if the announcer's voice is too loud and is distorting?

_____

6. Why are most radio and TV stations using cartridges for music instead of using records?

_____

_____

7. What is the difference between a "straight" and a production script for a radio commercial?

_____

_____

_____

8. Many times sound effects used in radio are not the real thing. The sound of rain drops, for example, can be produced by sprinkling rice on a drum. List two sound effects that can be produced artificially in the studio. What would you use to create them?

_____

_____

9. Why is it never a good idea to "get a level" of the talent by having him or her say "testing one-two-three"? What should be said?

_____

_____

_____

10. Generally how far should the announcer be from the microphone?

_____

Essay Question

(Use a separate sheet of paper for your response.)

It was said that radio would die after the coming of television Why does radio still exist today? How do they differ?

Chapter 5 Verbalizing the Message

1. Give three reasons why scripts are necessary for any good TV production.

_____

_____

_____

2. Briefly explain the difference in front timing and back timing a TV program.

_____

_____

_____

_____

3. Briefly explain the difference between "if cuts" and "cushions" when timing a TV production.

_____

_____

_____

_____

4. Give at least two examples of television programs that would be fully scripted.

_____

_____

5. Give at least two examples of television programs that would be partially scripted.

_____

_____

6. Instead of using a written script explaining the shots, many directors use a type of script that incorporates sketches to show what the camera operator is expected to shoot. What is the name of this type of script?

_____

7. Most TV scripts have two columns containing the necessary information. Name the two columns.

_____

_____

Name: _____ **Date:** _____

8. Why do most radio and TV stations use the services of ASCAP and BMI?

_____

_____

_____

9. Why is it difficult to present plays produced by your school on the local cable channel?

_____

_____

_____

10. The Television Code of the National Association of Broadcasters prohibits several things being shown on television. Give two examples of items not acceptable to the TV code.

_____

_____

Essay Question

(Use a separate sheet of paper for your response.)

Scripts not only help the talent verbalize the message, but also provide the technical staff information. What elements are included in a typical script? How do these elements help the technical staff produce the message?

Chapter 6   Producing the Message

1. Name the person who is responsible for the production and generally "calls the shots."

_____

2. Name the person in the studio responsible for giving the cues to all performers.

_____

3. Name the person in the control room who actually changes the cameras on the air.

_____

4. Name the person who is responsible for all sounds in the program.

_____

5. In many stations the camera operator will have a list of the shots he or she is expected to get during a telecast. What is this list called?

_____

6. Why is it necessary to "white balance" a camera before the production is taped?

_____

_____

_____

7. What is the difference between "head room" and "nose room" in TV shots?

_____

_____

_____

_____

8. Name the person who is responsible for the design and building of scenery for a telecast.

_____

9. Give an example where a mirror could be used to obtain a difficult shot during a TV program.

_____

Name: _____ Date: _____

10. Why do news anchors often hold scripts when they have TelePrompters?

_____

_____

_____

_____

Essay Question

(Use a separate sheet of paper for your response.)

You now have had some experience in TV production. Imagine that you are conducting a public-access course for a local cable company and are talking to a group of prospective camera operators. What eight suggestions would you give to these beginning camera operators? Explain why.

Chapter 7 Taping the Message

1. Videotape was invented in 1956. Until this time, what was the name of the recording device used to record TV programs?

_____

2. Give three advantages of videotape over a live TV program.

_____

_____

_____

3. Three separate recordings are made on videotape during recording. What are they?

_____

_____

_____

4. Why are many TV stations using "camcorders" for their news operations?

_____

_____

_____

_____

5. What is meant by the terms "pickups" and "reversals"?

_____

_____

_____

_____

6. Most TV news reports start with a "standup." What is meant by this term?

_____

_____

_____

_____

Name: _____ **Date:** _____

7. Why is a "crash edit" not as good as one made with a professional editor?

_____

_____

_____

8. Why is it a good idea for the announcer to give a countdown of 5-4-3-2 before starting any sequence on videotape?

_____

_____

_____

9. Why is it not a good idea to use the mike on top of many VCRs or on portable cameras for the audio in most productions?

_____

_____

_____

_____

10. What is meant by the term "wild video"? Give an example of when it would be used in a news story.

_____

_____

_____

_____

Essay Question

(Use a separate sheet of paper for your response.)

Explain the difference between assemble and insert edit. Give at least two examples of how each can be used in a TV production.

Chapter 8   Considering Careers in Television

Below are positions that help make most broadcast operations work. On a separate sheet of paper, briefly describe how each one ties into the broadcast field.

1. graphic artist

2. public relations person

3. lawyer

4. music librarian

5. researcher

6. maintenance engineer

7. station salesperson

8. public access coordinator

9. producer/director

10. news writer

Essay Question

(Use a separate sheet of paper for your response.)

There are many career avenues you can use to get into the broadcasting field. Some of them are mentioned in chapter 8 of *Television Production Today!* If your career interests lie in broadcasting, describe which area you would like to get involved in. Why did you choose this over others? Will this course help you to reach your career goals? Why or why not?

If your career interests lie elsewhere, explain what your future plans are. Why did you choose this over broadcasting? Will any of your television production skills be useful to you in your chosen field?

PART 8

Answer Key

Crossword Puzzle Answers

Chapter 1

Across

4. superstation
7. NBC
8. KOKA
9. DBS
10. FCC
11. Nielsen
12. prime

Down

1. spot
2. *Broadcasting*
3. zap
5. necessity
6. Fairness

Chapter 2

Across

2. canned
5. radio
6. receiver
8. AM

Down

1. decode
2. chroma
3. Pepsi
4. stage
7. ENG
9. minicams

Chapter 3

Across

4. Fresnel
5. shallow
7. Newvicon
9. tilt
10. cover
11. super
12. zoom

Down

1. subjective
2. dissolve
5. key
6. white
8. truck
10. cut
11. scoop

Chapter 4

Across

1. cart
2. mud
3. gain
4. cue
7. dynamic
8. board
10. ribbon

Down

1. cardioid
2. music
5. uni
6. lavaliere
9. pot

Chapter 5

Across

5. code
6. cold
7. copyright
10. story
12. news

Down

1. aspect
2. front
3. video
4. ASCAP
8. PIX
9. game
10. MS

Chapter 6

Across

1. tally
4. floor
6. audio
7. white
9. director
12. switcher
13. roll

Down

2. aperture
3. shot
5. ride
8. hod
10. talent
11. limbo

Chapter 7

Across	Down
3. insert	1. wild
6. heads	2. crash
7. assemble	4. reversal
10. camcorder	5. standup
	8. nose
	9. head

Chapter Test Answers

The page numbers in boldface type indicate where the answers appear in *Television Production Today!* Also included in this section are the comments on the Essay Questions.

Chapter 1

1. Any two of these: A.C. Nielsen, ARB, Trendex, Pulse **(page 7)**

2. Twelve **(page 9)**

3. KDKA, Pittsburg. It's still on the air. **(page 15)**

4. Reports on Hollywood stars, nutrition, health, soap operas, and film reviews are some examples cited. **(page 18)**

5. They are called "superstations" because satellites carry their programming far beyond their normal broadcast ranges. Examples include WGN, WOR, WTBS, and KTTV. **(page 6)**

6. Local origination programs are produced by the cable companies for the local communities. Public access programs are produced by the citizens themselves; the cable company simply airs the programs produced. **(page 11)**

7. Emotional appeals include: love for family, adventure, acquisition and savings, sex appeal, better taste, health, testimonials, use of humor, and pride. (You may have discussed even more.) **(page 26)**

8. *Broadcasting* magazine **(page 6, 26)**

9. Most people "zap" out the commercials when programs are recorded. **(page 8)**

10. There are differences in personal backgrounds, interests, prejudices, and knowledge. **(page 19)**

Essay Question

The following points should have been included in the essay whether the student perceived the technological growth in broadcasting as good or bad.

- Technology has created many more choices than in the past.
- It allows viewers opportunities for choosing their own types of recreational and informational programming.
- It allows for "narrow casting" (programs of special interest with limited appeal), which means those with special interests will be provided for.
- It creates problems with censorship and parent control.
- TV viewers are more informed than ever before.
- With pay TV, videotapes, and discs, the TV set has become the focal point of family recreation.

The students may have differing views on how television will affect the future, but their answers may include some of these points:

- Pay TV may replace local theatres as the main source of film viewing.
- With computers, discs, etc., television will become more than just an entertainment medium.
- Instructional and educational TV will become an important educational tool in schools.
- Communities will become active in cable programming.

Allow them to "prophesize"—as long as their predictions are based on some of the material in Chapter 1.

Chapter 2

1. Radio allows for more creativity. One is not restricted on radio. Costumes, sets, and makeup are not needed on radio. **(page 38)**

2. Here are some of the differences between performing on television and performing on stage. **(pages 33-34)**

a. Those who perform on stage have an audience. Those who perform on TV usually do not have an audience.

b. The audience in a stage production sits throughout. In TV, the audience can come and go as it pleases.

c. In TV, the audience "sees" only what the director wants him or her to see.

d. The director on TV has constant control of the situation. In a stage production it is out of the director's hands once the play starts.

3. Chroma key allows for visuals to be inserted behind the anchor, allowing for a more visual effect. **(page 37)**

4. Radio is called "theatre of the mind" because the entire setting—including costumes, makeup, and so on—is in the mind of the listener. He or she makes it up as the broadcast takes place. **(page 38)**

5. Videotape is much faster. There is no processing time for tape. It can be transmitted immediately from a minicam truck to the station. Film has to be sent to a processing lab before it can be sent to the TV station. **(pages 41–42)**

6. FM is static free and is created for high fidelity. **(page 40)**

7. The third element is sound effects. Only the voice, music, and sound effects can be presented on radio. **(page 38)**

8. ENG stands for Electronic News Gathering. **(page 42)**

9. An announcer should think he or she is talking to only one person at a time. This is because normally there is only one person in the room or in the car who is listening to the radio. It is important to make them feel the announcer is talking directly to them. **(page 47)**

10. The three parts shown in the communication model include: the sender, the message, and the receiver. **(page 43)**

Essay Question

If the students picked radio to sell the product, these are some of the points they should have mentioned in the essay:

- Radio commercials generally reach more people.
- Radio commercials are less expensive.
- Radio commercials should play on the listener's imagination.
- Radio commercials should use sound effects and music.
- Radio commercials are less expensive to produce than a TV spot.

If they picked television, these are some of the points the students should have mentioned:

- TV is visual. This can be used as an advantage (food looks great and appealing on TV).
- In TV, the script will rely more on non-verbal cues.
- It is said, "A picture is worth a thousand words." Use pictures of the product to sell.
- Elaborate use of costumes and film techniques can hold a viewer's attention.
- MTV-type commercials are being used to get younger viewers to buy products (note McDonald's, Burger King, and Levis 501 Jeans).

Chapter 3

1. a. Vidicon: Advantages—inexpensive, rugged, lasts long.
Disadvantages—poor under low light, tends to turn green, lags. **(page 53)**

b. Saticon™: Advantages—picture detail is better, color resolution much better, needs less light.
Disadvantages—more expensive, less rugged. **(pages 54-55)**

c. Newvicon®: Advantages—better resolution, best picture under low light, will not lag or burn in.
Disadvantages—more expensive, tends to lose color under lower light. **(page 54)**

2. Depth of focus is the distance between the lens and the subject on camera. The depth of field is the area around the subject that is in focus. Remember, the depth of field relies in part on the depth of focus. **(pages 62-63)**

3.
a. truck right **(pages 64,65)**

b. arc left **(page 64)**

c. dolly out **(page 64)**

d. tilt up **(pages 64, 65)**

e. pan left **(page 64)**

4. A high angle shot (shooting down) **(page 70)**

5. A telephoto lens is better because it tends to flatten the picture and make the cars appear to be closer together, creating traffic jams on the screen. **(pages 60-61)**

6. An objective shot creates the illusion the audience is viewing the scene apart from the situation. We view the situation objectively. A subjective shot makes the viewer a character in the story. The camera actually becomes a character in the story. **(page 64)**

7. A floor plan is necessary to save time during rehearsals or productions. All of the necessary details can be worked out ahead of time. Remember, technicians standing around costs money. Items included in a standard floor plan include: cameras and angles, lights, sets, talent locations, mike locations, and furniture location. **(page 88)**

8. Three point lighting consists of key, back, and fill lights. **(pages 93-94)**

9. Dimension can be created by doing several things. Choose any three of the following. **(page 74)**

a. Shoot action from many angles.

b. Have the performers move around.

c. Move the cameras.

d. Use short depth of field shots.

e. Use gradient lines in the sets (shoot in corners).

f. Place smaller objects near the camera.

g. Use three point lighting.

10. Aspect ratio is 4 units wide by 3 units high. **(page 78)**

Essay Question

Here are some visual suggestions the students might use for the raspberry-flavored soft drink commercial.

- Use fresh fruits in the visuals.

- Pick visuals showing how the soft drink will quench thirst.

- Use visuals showing young people enjoying the soft drink. Think of situations where this soft drink would fit in such as teen parties, etc.

- Use vibrant colors that will help sell the soft drink.

- Close-up of the soft drink (with condensation on the glass). The hot yellow/orange sun in the background.

- Shots of people taking a break from a game (soccer) and quenching their thirst with the soft drink.

- Shots of a person dancing on roller skates and holding a bottle of the soft drink in one hand.

The students should explain why they chose a certain type of visual. For example, if the student wants to convey that the soft drink is made from natural-flavored raspberry, the use of fruits in the commercial would be appropriate. The purpose of this essay is to show students that in television, visuals play a significant role in selling the product.

Chapter 4

1.
a. Unidirectional: The pick up pattern is live only on one side. All other sides are dead. **(pages 114-115)**

b. Bidirectional: Two sides are live, two sides are dead. It is great for interviews. **(page 115)**

c. Omnidirectional: All sides are live. **(page 115)**

d. Cardioid: Pick up pattern is in the shape of a heart (very much like unidirectional except that the pattern narrows as one goes farther from the mike. **(page 115)**

2.
a. Dynamic mike is the best (filters out wind, etc.). **(page 116)**

b. A condensor mike is used for lavalieres as they can make them very small. **(page 117)**

c. A PZM® can pick up sound from great distances and from all angles. It would be the best if only one could be used. **(page 117)**

3. a. Board: A mixer which allows one person to mix mikes, records, carts, etc. from one source. **(pages 122-123)**

b. Pot: Short for potentiometer. It controls the volume level for mikes, etc. **(page 124)**

c. Cart: Short for cartridge or cartridge recorder. **(pages 131-132)**

d. VU meter: Volume Unit meter. Used to measure the volume of the output of the audio board. **(page 123)**

4. Even though the announcer may not be seen on radio, he or she gestures and uses facial expressions in order to create the idea that communication is taking place. A good announcer imagines he or she is talking to people, not to a microphone. **(pages 126-127)**

5. a. If the announcer is too low he or she is said to be "in the mud." **(page 124)**

b. If the announcer is too loud he or she is "bending the needle" or "pinning the needle." **(page 124)**

6. Cartridges are now used for music because they do not warp or scratch and are instantly cued. **(page 132)**

7. A straight script means that an announcer reads from the script with no use of sound effects or music. A production, or situation, commercial also uses characters, music, and sound effects. **(pages 136–138)**

8. Choose any two of the following. More are listed in this chapter. **(page 131)**

- monkeys—rubbing wet cork against the bottle opening.
- bones breaking—chewing candy mints or celery close to the mike.
- fire—crackling cellophane near the mike.

9. You want the talent to read what he or she is going to read on the air or to talk with the announcer. This way, the audio technician can obtain an average VU level. Then there is no surprise when the talent speaks on the air. **(page 121)**

10. An announcer should read 8 to 10 inches away from the microphone. **(page 122)**

Essay Question

Radio exists today because it satisfies a different need. Radio appeals to people on the go or busy doing other things, whereas television demands more attention from the viewers. To compete with television, radio generally broadcasts music, news, and talk shows.

They differ in that:

- radio is often just in the background. No real attention is needed. This allows those listening to radio to do other things.
- radio is geared more for local audiences. There are many more local radio stations in the country than TV stations.
- radio concentrates on music rather than visual entertainment.
- radio concentrates on one listener at a time. The major listener is at home or in the car on the way to or from work.
- radio is more up to date. News stories can easily be broadcast on the air on radio. TV relies on the visual element of the story. All it takes is a phone booth to get a news story on radio.

Chapter 5

1. Scripts are necessary **(page 159)**:

a. to provide smooth introductions and conclusions.

b. to provide for accurate timing.

c. to provide the technical staff with the necessary information to get the production running as smoothly as possible.

2. Front timing gives the timing from the beginning of the program or segment to the end. It gives the time it goes on the air and the time it is to go off. Back timing means timing the program from the end; how much time is left in the segment. It means counting backward. **(pages 172-173)**

3. "If cuts" are parts that can be omitted if time runs out. Cushions are materials that can be added if a program is too short. **(page 160)**

4. Fully scripted programs include plays, newscasts, commercials, and political talks. **(page 161)**

5. Partially scripted shows include interviews, demonstrations, play-by-play sports, game shows. **(pages 162-163)**

6. storyboard (**page 169**)

7. video and audio (**page 166**)

8. ASCAP and BMI license all music played on the air. (**page 176**)

9. Copyright agreements must be made before any play is presented in public. (**page 176**)

10. According to the NAB Code, several items are prohibited. (**pages 178-179**)

   a. Profanity and obscenity are prohibited.

   b. Words derisive of any race, color, creed, or nationality are to be avoided.

   c. Presentations of techniques of crime in detail should not give ideas to others.

   d. There should be no act of hypnosis, lottery, legal, or medical advice.

   e. There should be no use of bulletins that might be taken as true.

Essay Question

A typical script includes the following:

- All pictures to be shown during the telecast. Exactly what will the viewer "see."
- All audio cues to be given. What will be said by the talent during the program; what music will be used.
- What camera will get what shot?
- All instructions to be given by the director.
- Special instructions, such as off-camera remarks, cue from videotape, etc.
- What shots are expected by each camera operator.
- Special instructions for the floor crew.
- Special instructions for the videotape operator ("roll tape").

These instructions on the script help the crew decide what its job will be while the director concentrates on preparing the studio, etc. The camera operators can set their shots while the others are working with talent, etc. The audio technician can cue music, set mikes, etc. It allows each person responsible to determine, ahead of time, what is to be done. This saves time and money during a production.

Chapter 6

1. director (**pages 213, 227**)

2. floor or stage manager (**pages 214-215**)

3. switcher or technical director (**pages 225-226**)

4. audio technician (**pages 221-222**)

5. shot chart (**page 217**)

6. Color TV cameras must be told what "white" looks like under various lighting conditions. If white is truly white, then the other colors will, in all probability, be true. (**pages 216-217**)

7. Head room is the space above the talent's head and the top of the screen. It is important to have a little room at the top as some TV sets are not adjusted and the person's head may appear to be cut off. Nose room is the space in front of a person as he or she faces right or left. (**page 220**)

8. art director (**page 224**)

9. getting an overview shot of a typewriter keyboard (**page 229**)

10. Most anchors hold scripts for two reasons. 1) The TelePrompter may suddenly present problems. 2) Often the anchor has more credibility if he or she holds a script. This way it does not appear that the anchor is making up what he or she is saying. (**pages 237-238**)

Essay Question

Here are the eight suggestions one would give to beginning camera operators:

- Do not frame a shot too tightly.
- Wait for the director's cues to change shots. Do not "fish" for your own shots.
- Pan and tilt very slowly. "Swish pans" are very distracting.
- Allow "head room" at the top of the screen. But do not allow too much or a person would look funny growing out at the bottom of a TV screen.
- Never have half of a person in a shot. For example, a 2-shot consists of two people— not a person and an elbow of another.

- Do not zoom in or out constantly during a program.
- Check composition. A plant in the background may appear to be growing out of the talent's head in the camera.
- Keep the camera still. Jerky camera movements are distracting.

Chapter 7

1. Kinescope recordings (films made off a TV screen) were used before videotape. **(page 248)**

2. There are many advantages of tape. Here are some. A complete list appears in the text. **(page 250)**

    a. It makes delayed broadcasts possible.

    b. It makes scheduling programs easier.

    c. It provides for remote broadcasts outside the studio.

    d. It provides for more efficient use of staff time.

    e. It can provide for editing and updating material.

    f. Mistakes can be edited out of a program or segment.

    g. It can be played back many times.

    h. It can be erased and used over again.

3. Three recordings are made at the same time: 1) audio 2) video, and 3) a control track. **(page 269)**

4. Camcorders are smaller and more convenient to carry, as the recorder and camera are together. In addition, it provides for one less crew member, since someone is not needed to carry the recorder along with a camera. **(pages 259-260)**

5. "Pickups" and "reversals" are recorded on tape after the interview is taped with one camera. After the interview is finished, the crew will get a shot of the reporter from the opposite angle and edit the shot into the interview later. They "pickup" the shot after the interview. **(page 266)**

6. The "standup" refers to the fact that the reporter often begins the story standing in front of a building or place that is identified with the story. A reporter may stand in front of the main gate to begin a report on a prison break. **(page 267)**

7. Crash edits accomplished by using the pause button often show glitches and lose sync, causing a rolling on the screen. **(pages 270-271)**

8. A countdown by the announcer or reporter will help the tape editor edit the tape by giving audible cues. **(page 268)**

9. Most recorders allow for a separate mike to be used, allowing for better audio reproduction. The mike on the camera is generally not used because the reporter stands too far away. He or she sounds off mike. **(page 266)**

10. Wild video is a term for video shots that can be inserted later. For example, if a reporter interviews a coach about an upcoming game, it is a good idea to shoot part of the practice before or after the interview. This wild video can be then inserted in the interview to avoid talking heads. **(page 266)**

Essay Question

Assemble edits are used to "piece a story together." It allows the editor and reporter to stop the tape after one sequence, go to another, and continue. The assemble edit allows the editor to keep adding new elements to the story. Two examples of assemble edits:

- A drama with scene changes. The scene takes place in one location. Then suddenly, the drama takes place somewhere else.
- One news reporter may cover one part of a story in one location and then cut to another reporter somewhere else.

Insert edits allow the editor to add new pictures in the middle of an existing story. The visuals may be changed and then the editor may go back to original picture without a "glich" in the picture. Here are some examples of how insert edits can be used:

- Wild video, shot after an interview, can be placed in the middle of the interview to avoid "talking heads."
- Shots of the reporter taking notes can be placed in the middle of a news conference story.
- New commercials can be inserted in old TV programs without destroying the content.
- In music videos, inserts allow for editing without destroying the original sound track.

Chapter 8

1. Graphic artist. Graphic artists create logos for TV stations, create courtroom drawings where cameras are not permitted, create cartoons for news stories, and create visual effects for commercial products. **(pages 284-285, 292)**

2. Public relations person. Most TV stations employ public relations persons to promote the station's activities. Local newspapers carry ads by TV stations promoting the 11 PM newscast. These TV ads, as well as radio spots, are created by the public relations department. The public relations people help TV stations relate to local communities. They arrange for tours and help local groups use the radio or TV station for publicity. **(page 283)**

3. Lawyer. Most radio and TV stations employ lawyers on their staff. They are needed to guard against statements that may be libelous and that might create a lawsuit against the station. In addition, lawyers help stations prepare evidence for its license renewal by the FCC. TV and radio stations also need lawyers to defend them against FCC actions. The FCC need lawyers to determine rulings in all aspects of broadcasting. Local cable companies utilize lawyers to write franchises for the local communities. These lawyers also may check on copyright infringement. **(pages 289-290)**

4. Music librarian. Many large radio and TV stations employ a music librarian to catalog, store, and find music needed for broadcasting. This person is responsible for all the music played on a station. A disk jockey or program director would come to the music director and ask him or her to find music written by a particular artist, a certain theme, or a mood needed for a story or a commercial. The music director helps the programming department find any music needed for on-air playing. **(pages 290, 291)**

5. Researcher. Many news departments hire researchers to help with editorials, commentaries, and news stories. The research staff will do background stories on local news items, freeing reporters to concentrate on the immediate aspect of the story. Research staffers may do the necessary research for background. Many commentators have a research staff do the leg work for them in writing commentaries. Game shows have research teams to look for questions and answers to use on the air. **(pages 293-294)**

6. Maintenance engineer. The equipment used by radio and TV stations is expensive and often delicate. Engineers are needed to keep all the equipment in good working condition. If a video recorder breaks down in the middle of a newscast, this could cause disaster. In addition, the transmitters must be maintained and kept in good operating condition as inspected by the FCC. Engineers also help design, purchase, and maintain satellite systems needed to receive programming from networks and news sources. **(page 289)**

7. Salesperson. A radio or TV station only makes money if people buy commercial time on the station. Salespersons are needed to persuade local or national businesses to purchase commercial time on the radio or TV station. These salespersons also help the local or national businesses plan the commercials to be used on the air. **(pages 285-286)**

8. Public access coordinator. Many communities or cable TV companies hire a public access coordinator to help local access users utilize the public access channel for the cable company. These persons help schedule programs on the access channels. In addition, they plan classes so local cable users know what kinds of programs can be produced. The access coordinator helps schedule the use of the remote vans, access equipment, and studio time and space. Many communities are hiring access coordinators to help the local groups plan and produce local access programming. **(pages 296-297)**

9. Producer/director. Producers and directors are not only needed for TV stations, but they also are needed to produce programs for cable companies, college stations, industrial companies, and advertising agencies. **(pages 283, 291)**

10. News writer. Most people do not realize that the anchors do not write what is said during the newscast. The introductions to stories is written for them by writers. They work with producers and tape editors to write the stories that are seen or heard on the air on both the local and network TV newscasts. **(pages 294-295)**

Essay Question

The answers for this essay relies on the students' interests and future plans. Hopefully, they will have used ideas from the text and from class to help them in their choices. This is also a good chance for students to express their constructive opinions about the course.

LANGUAGE ARTS BOOKS

Business Communication
Business Communication Today!, *Thomas and Fryar*
Effective Group Communication, *Ratliffe and Stech*
Handbook for Business Writing, *Baugh, Fryar and Thomas*
Successful Business Speaking, *Fryar and Thomas*
Successful Business Writing, *Sitzmann*
Successful Interviewing, *Sitzmann and Garcia*
Successful Problem Solving, *Fryar and Thomas*
Working in Groups, *Ratliffe and Stech*

Reading
Building Real Life English Skills, *Penn and Starkey*
English Survival Series, *Maggs*
Essential Life Skills Series, *Penn and Starkey*
Everyday Consumer English, *Kleinman and Weissman*
Literature Alive!, *Gamble and Gamble*
Practical Skills in Reading, *Keech and Sanford*
Reading by Doing, *Simmons and Palmer*

Grammar
Essentials of English Grammar, *Baugh*
Grammar Step-By-Step Vol. 1, *Pratt*
Grammar Step-By-Step Vol. 2, *Pratt*

Speech
Contemporary Speech, *HopKins and Whitaker*
Creative Speaking, *Buys et al.*
Creative Speaking Series, *Buys et al.*
Getting Started in Public Speaking, *Prentice and Payne*
Listening by Doing, *Galvin*
Literature Alive!, *Gamble and Gamble*
Person to Person, *Galvin and Book*
Person to Person Workbook, *Galvin and Book*
Self-Awareness, *Ratliffe and Herman*
Speaking by Doing, *Buys, Sill and Beck*

Journalism
Journalism Today!, *Ferguson and Patten*
The Journalism Today! Workbook, *Ferguson and Patten*

Media
Media, Messages & Language, *McLuhan, Hutchon and McLuhan*
Photography in Focus, *Jacobs and Kokrda*
Television Production Today!, *Kirkham*
The Mass Media Workbook, *Hollister*
Understanding Mass Media, *Schrank*
Understanding the Film, *Johnson and Bone*

Theatre
Acting and Directing, *Grandstaff*
An Introduction to Theatre and Drama, *Cassady and Cassady*
Dynamics of Acting, *Snyder and Drumstra*
Play Production Today!, *Beck et al.*
Stagecraft, *Beck*
The Book of Scenes for Acting Practice, *Cassady*

Mythology
Great Myths and Epics, *Rosenberg*
Mythology and You, *Rosenberg and Baker*
World Mythology: An Anthology of Great Myths and Epics, *Rosenberg*

Genre Literature
The Detective Story, *Schwartz*
The Short Story and You, *Simmons and Stern*
You and Science Fiction, *Hollister*

Language, Writing and Composition
An Anthology for Young Writers, *Meredith*
Lively Writing, *Schrank*
Look, Think & Write!, *Leavitt and Sohn*
Snap, Crackle & Write, *Schrank*
Tandem: Language in Action Series
    Action/Interaction, *Dufour and Strauss*
    Point/Counterpoint, *Dufour and Strauss*
The Art of Composition, *Meredith*
The Book of Forms for Everyday Living, *Rogers*
Writing in Action, *Meredith*
Writing by Doing, *Sohn and Enger*

For further information or a current catalog, write:
National Textbook Company
4255 West Touhy Avenue
NTC Lincolnwood, Illinois 60646-1975 U.S.A.